American Lives

Samuel Adams

Jennifer Blizin Gillis

Heinemann Library
Chicago, Illinois

© 2005 Heinemann Library
a division of Reed Elsevier Inc.
Chicago, Illinois

Customer Service 888-454-2279
Visit our website at www.heinemannlibrary.com

Designed by Heinemann Library
Photo research by Heather Sabel
Printed and bound in China by WKT Company
Limited

09 08 07 06 05
10 9 8 7 6 5 4 3 2 1

Library of Congress Cataloging-in-Publication Data
Gillis, Jennifer Blizin, 1950-
   Samuel Adams / Jennifer Blizin Gillis.
      v. cm. -- (American lives)
   Includes bibliographical references and index.
   Contents: The happiest morning -- Early years --
Samuel at school -- Poor Adams -- Sad times -- Life
in politics -- Writing and fighting -- The most
dangerous man -- From bad to worse -- Tea
overboard! -- To arms -- The Revolutionary War --
Last days.
   ISBN 1-4034-5962-2 (HC), 1-4034-5970-3 (pbk.)
 1. Adams, Samuel, 1722-1803--Juvenile literature.
2. Politicians--United States--Biography--Juvenile
literature. 3. Revolutionaries--United States--
Biography--Juvenile literature. 4. United States.
Declaration of Independence--Signers--Biography--
Juvenile literature. 5. United States--History--
Revolution, 1775-1783--Biography--Juvenile
literature. [1. Adams, Samuel, 1722-1803. 2.
Politicians. 3. United States--History--Revolution,
1775-1783.] I. Title. II. Series: American lives
(Heinemann Library (Firm))

E302.6.A2G55 2004
973.3'092--dc22
                                  2003027787

Acknowledgments
The author and publishers are grateful to the
following for permission to reproduce copyright
material:

Cover photograph by Bettmann/Corbis

Title page, pp. 8-10, 14, 15, 20, 21 The Granger
Collection, New York; pp. 4, 25 Hulton
Archive/Getty Images; p. 5 Corbis; p. 7 Burstein
Collection/Corbis; p. 11 The Corcoran Gallery of
Art/Corbis; p. 12 W. H. Parish/Haley & Steele; pp.
13, 16 North Wind Picture Archives; pp. 17, 23
Bettmann/Corbis; p. 18 Library of Congress; p. 19
Jerry Shulman/SuperStock; p. 22 Kevin
Fleming/Corbis; pp. 24, 27 National Archives and
Records Administration; p. 26 Lee Snider/Corbis;
p. 28 New York Public Library/Art Resource; p.29l
Art Resource; p. 29r Richard T. Nowitz/Corbis

The publisher would like to thank Michelle Rimsa
for her comments in the preparation of this book.

The cover image of Samuel Adams was painted while
he was governor of Massachusetts.

Contents

Some words are shown in bold, **like this.** You can find out what they mean by looking in the glossary.

A Glorious Morning

It was April 18, 1775. The British wanted to capture Samuel Adams. For years, he had wanted American **colonists** to fight for independence from Great Britain. Now, he was hiding in Lexington, Massachusetts, near Boston. After midnight, a rider named Paul Revere came to tell Samuel to leave. British soldiers were coming.

At dawn, British troops marched toward a small group of American **patriot** soldiers in the center of town. After repeated orders from the soldiers, some colonists began to leave. But suddenly, Samuel heard a gunshot.

Samuel Adams was called the father of American revolution and American independence. He spent his whole adult life working to free America from Great Britain.

No one knows who fired the first shot at Lexington, but it was called "the shot heard 'round the world" because it began the Revolutionary War.

The British were shooting at the patriots! The **Revolutionary War** had started. There was no turning back. Americans would fight to be free, or die trying. Later, Samuel told his friends that this was "a glorious morning."

Early Years

Samuel Adams was born on September 27, 1722. His father made malt, which was used to make vinegar and beer. He also took part in town **politics.** Samuel often spent time listening to his father and his friends talking about government.

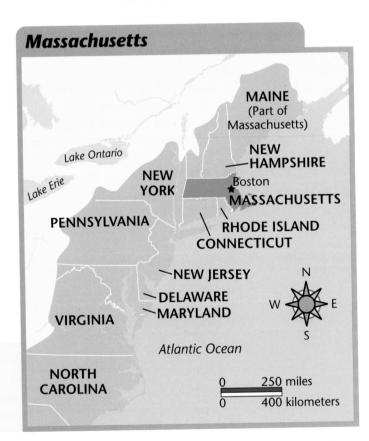

Massachusetts

Lake Ontario

Lake Erie

NEW YORK

PENNSYLVANIA

MAINE (Part of Massachusetts)

NEW HAMPSHIRE

Boston

MASSACHUSETTS

RHODE ISLAND

CONNECTICUT

NEW JERSEY

DELAWARE

MARYLAND

VIRGINIA

Atlantic Ocean

NORTH CAROLINA

N W E S

0   250 miles
0   400 kilometers

Samuel was born in Boston, Massachusetts.

The Life of Samuel Adams

1722	1749	1757	1764
Born at noon on September 27 in Boston, Massachusetts	Marries Elizabeth Checkley	Elizabeth dies	Marries Elizabeth "Betsy" Wells

As a boy, Samuel often watched the ships in Boston Harbor from the roof of his house. This old drawing shows the harbor in those days.

Both of Samuel's parents were very religious and involved in their church. They believed in working hard, living simply, and getting along with their neighbors. All of his life, Samuel believed in these things, too.

Samuel had eleven brothers and sisters, but in those days many children died from diseases. Samuel's older sister Mary and his younger brother Joseph were the only other children in the family who lived to be adults.

1774	**1775**	**1794**	**1803**
Selected to represent Massachusetts at First **Continental Congress**	*Samuel almost captured just before battle of Lexington*	*Elected governor of Massachusetts*	*Dies at home in Boston on October 2*

Samuel at School

When he was seven years old, Samuel started school. He went to the Grammar School of Boston. He was a very good student, and his parents hoped that he would become a minister. At his graduation, he gave a speech in **Latin.**

Samuel went to Harvard College when he was fourteen years old. He was serious about his schoolwork. He studied Greek, Latin, and **Hebrew.**

This is how many schools in Boston looked around the time Samuel was a young boy.

In Samuel's day, Harvard College was a place where men studied to be ministers. No women were allowed to go there.

While he was at Harvard, Samuel became interested in law and **politics.** He read a book by a man named John Locke. Locke thought that the government's job was to protect people's rights and property. These ideas made Samuel disagree with the way the British treated the colonies.

What Did He Look Like?

There are no pictures of Samuel as a young man. People who knew him then said he was about medium height and had a large head. He had dark eyes and always looked at people with a kind expression.

"Poor Adams"

After he left Harvard, Samuel Adams began studying to become a lawyer. He soon changed his mind. Then he got a job as a clerk. Adams the good student was not a good worker! He spent his lunch hours in **taverns** talking **politics,** and he was often late getting back to work. After only a few months, Adams left his job. He may have been fired.

Adams and his friends started a club to talk about politics. They printed a newspaper called the *Public Advertiser.* Adams wrote pieces for the paper about the rights of people.

Adams worked as a clerk in a countinghouse like this one. It was like working in a bank.

This painting shows a wealthy man of the 1700s. In those days, wealthy people in Boston copied the styles that British people wore.

His father gave him one thousand British pounds to start a business. Today, that would be worth about $160,000. But Adams lent most of it to a friend, who never paid him back. People in Boston started calling Samuel "Poor Adams," because it seemed that he would never get a job or make any money. Adams dressed very simply and wore clothes until they fell apart before buying new ones.

Sad Times

In 1748, Samuel Adams's father died. Samuel took over the malt business, but he was not very good at it. One year later, his mother died.

Adams married Elizabeth Checkley in 1749. They were married for eight years. Elizabeth died in 1757. Then, the Adams family malt business failed.

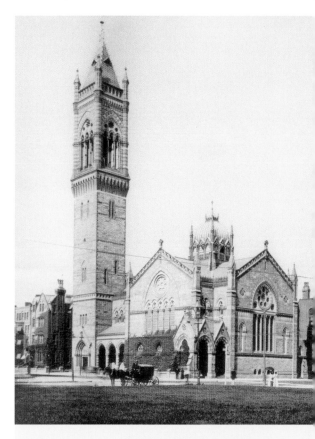

Elizabeth Checkley's father was minister of New South Church, which was around the corner from the Adams home.

Samuel's Children

Samuel and Elizabeth had five or six children, but only two of them lived to be adults.

- *Samuel, born 1751*
- *Hannah, born 1756*

MILITIA CROSSING THE MOUNTAINS.

During the time Adams was working through problems in his personal life, there was a war going on in North America. It was called the French and Indian War (1754-1763). Some American colonists fought with the British Army against the French.

The General Court ordered the town sheriff to take away Adams's house to pay debts Samuel's father owed. Adams printed an advertisement in the newspaper. It said he would **sue** anyone who tried buy his property. Luckily, no one tried.

Life in Politics

Soon after Samuel Adams married, he began to take part in Boston **politics.** First, he was elected to be the town trash collector.

In 1756, he was elected to be Boston's **tax** collector. This was an important but dangerous job. If tax collectors were not able to get the money people owed the town, they had to pay it themselves.

Many people came to town meetings. Sometimes they got so angry about politics that fights broke out in the town hall!

The King of England chose Thomas Hutchinson to be governor of Massachusetts. He and Adams were lifelong enemies. Hutchinson thought Adams was always trying to start trouble.

Adams was not a good tax collector because he never forced anyone to pay. Sometimes he just collected a little of what people really owed. By 1764, he was thousands of pounds behind in collecting taxes. The governor said Adams was stealing the tax money, but this was not true. At a town meeting, Adams apologized for being a bad tax collector. The people of Boston elected him to be tax collector again.

Around this time, Adams began seeing Elizabeth Wells. She was the daughter of one of his father's friends. They married in December, 1764. He called her "Betsy."

Writing and Fighting

When Adams was in his forties, most people thought he was a failure. He had lost his family business. He had no money. He dressed in old clothes. But it was Adams who planted the seeds that grew into the **Revolutionary War.** Adams made independence for the **colonies** his job.

To raise money, Great Britain put **taxes** on things the colonists used. Adams began to write newspaper articles and letters that said the taxes were unfair. His wife said she often fell asleep at night to the sound of his pen scratching on paper.

Great Britain put a tax on almost every piece of paper the colonists bought. Each one had to have a stamp on it, like this one. Even playing cards had to have a stamp on them.

A STAMP.

Calling All Patriots

*Samuel Adams's younger cousin John Adams later became president of the United States. John wrote that Samuel made a habit of making friends with young men, warning them about Great Britain, and encouraging them to join the **patriots.***

Green Dragon Tavern, Boston, Mass., in 1773

Working people often went to the Green Dragon **tavern.** Adams spent so much time in taverns that his enemies began calling him "Sam the Publican." *Publican* had a double meaning. It was Latin for "of the people," and *pub* was another name for a tavern.

Adams was a good talker, too. He organized farmers, fishers, and other working people into a group called the Sons of Liberty. The group organized **protests** against taxes. Adams talked wealthy men such as John Hancock, Joseph Warren, and Josiah Quincy into working for independence. Other cities began having Sons of Liberty meetings, too.

The Most Dangerous Man

Great Britain ended the Stamp **Tax** in 1766. To celebrate, people had parties and fireworks. Adams worried that **colonists** would forget about their problems with Great Britain and stop working for independence. But before long, Great Britain added taxes on more things.

By now, Adams was a lawmaker in the Massachusetts House of **Representatives.** They sent a letter written by Adams to the other twelve colonies. It said that no one should tax the American colonists but other Americans. It also asked the colonists to boycott, or stop buying, things from Great Britain.

Adams used false names, such as "Vindex" or "Candidus," when he wrote. But most people had a good idea who was speaking out against the British.

Adams had a Newfoundland dog like this one. People who knew Adams said that he taught the dog to bark at and bite British soldiers.

The governor was furious when he heard about the letter. He asked for a warship to be sent to Boston Harbor to keep an eye on the city. He asked to have soldiers in Boston to stop **protests.**

Adams wrote more newspaper articles about the new taxes. He complained about the British soldiers and reminded the people of Boston not to buy things that came from England. The governor at the time called Adams "the most dangerous man in Massachusetts," because he never stopped speaking out against Great Britain.

From Bad to Worse

In 1768, Adams started a new newspaper. He worried that people in other **colonies** would not care about what was happening in Boston. So he made up stories about horrible things British soldiers did to ordinary people in Boston.

Boston was getting dangerous. In 1770, British soldiers fired their guns into a crowd of angry colonists. Adams told Governor Hutchinson that he must order the soldiers to leave Boston. After that, the British called these soldiers "the Sam Adams **Regiments.**"

When British soldiers fired into a crowd of colonists, five people died. **Patriots** called this the Boston Massacre, meaning that the soldiers had fired their guns for no reason.

Adams and his wealthy friend John Hancock later became friends again. Hancock was so happy that he had this picture of Adams painted. Adams was about 50 years old then.

When the soldiers left Boston, people calmed down. They wanted to make peace with the British, but Adams wanted them to keep working for independence. Some of his friends, including John Hancock, thought he was wrong. Suddenly, Adams was not very popular.

Tea Overboard!

Things did not stay calm for long. In 1773, Great Britain put a **tax** on tea—the most popular drink in the **colonies.** Samuel Adams talked people into boycotting, or refusing to buy, British tea. When three tea ships arrived in November, the people of Boston would not buy any of the tea.

Adams and the people of Boston met in this church on December 16, 1773. All day, Adams and other people made speeches about Great Britain's taxes.

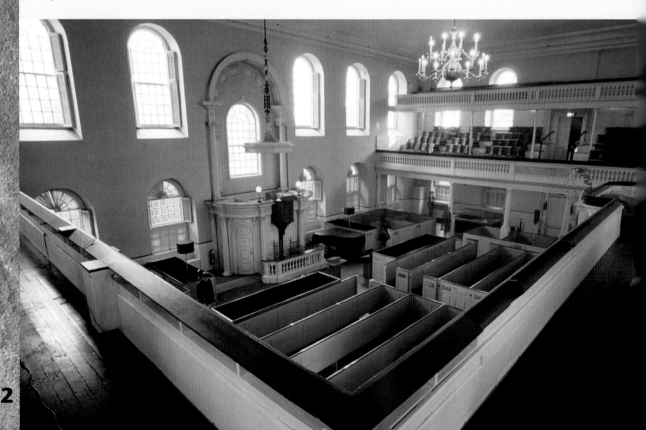

This old drawing shows the Sons of Liberty throwing tea into Boston Harbor. They dressed as Native Americans so no one would know who they were. Soon, other colonies were having "tea parties" like this one.

On December 16, the tea ships were still in the harbor. The people of Boston met all day to decide what to do. One of the ships' captains was there. That evening, Adams sent him to ask Governor Hutchinson to let the ships leave Boston without unloading the tea.

The governor refused. When he heard this, Adams gave a secret signal. Suddenly, some of the Sons of Liberty ran to Boston Harbor and climbed onto the tea ships. They threw all of the tea into the water.

To Arms

Great Britain punished the city of Boston for the tea party. They thought this would scare all the **colonies** into calming down. The king sent warships to close Boston Harbor. This made it hard for people to get food or supplies. He ordered British soldiers to stay in people's homes. The townspeople had to feed them.

Adams wrote letters to other colonies to make sure they knew what was happening in Boston. He and a **patriot** named Benjamin Franklin decided that lawmakers from each colony should meet.

Adams's trip to Philadelphia was the first time he had ever been out of Massachusetts. His friends wanted him to look good, so they surprised him with a trunk full of new clothes just before he left Boston.

Lawmakers from different colonies had never worked together before the First Continental Congress.

This meeting, called the first **Continental Congress,** took place in Philadelphia, Pennsylvania, in 1774. The lawmakers were angry with Great Britain, but most did not want to fight. Adams and a **patriot** named Patrick Henry led a group that wanted independence. At last, Congress decided that each colony should begin organizing groups of soldiers for war. They voted to stop buying anything from Great Britain.

The Revolutionary War

When the British heard about the First **Continental Congress,** they were angry. They blamed Adams for all the trouble. They wanted to send soldiers to find and capture or kill Adams and other **patriot** leaders. But

Adams and his friend John Hancock stayed at this house on the first night of the Battle of Lexington.

Adams went on writing letters and newspaper articles about independence from Great Britain.

Just before the second Continental Congress, some friends heard that the British were going to try to capture Adams. They told him to leave Boston for Lexington, Massachusetts. He could wait there until it was time to leave for Philadelphia. While he was there, the **Revolutionary War** started.

In 1776 Adams signed the **Declaration of Independence.** Now the thirteen colonies were the United States of America. But the new country's army was small and poor. During the war, Adams worked hard to get money and supplies for the U.S. soldiers.

The Revolutionary War lasted six years. On October 19, 1781, the British surrendered to General George Washington at Yorktown, Virginia.

Last Days

After the war, Samuel Adams wanted to retire. But his country still needed his help. In 1788 Adams helped write the Bill of Rights, a paper that promises certain rights to all Americans. Six years later, Adams was elected governor of Massachusetts. He was reelected two times.

As he got older, Adams liked to talk only about things that had happened in the years before the **Revolutionary War,** such as the Stamp **Tax** and the Boston Tea Party.

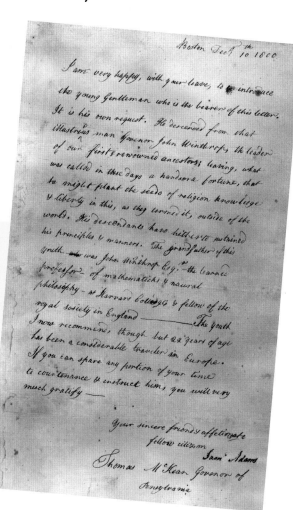

When Adams was older, he had a disease that made his head, hands, and voice shake. His granddaughter Elizabeth often wrote his letters, and Adams would sign them.

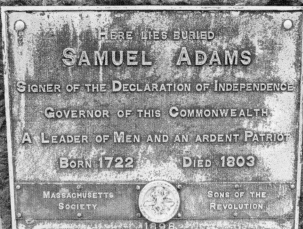

This sign marks Adams's grave at the Old Granary Burial Ground in Boston.

Sometime around his 81st birthday, Adams told his family and friends that he did not want a fancy funeral. He died a few days later on October 2, 1803. On the day of his funeral all the stores in Boston closed. Church bells rang and ships in the harbor lowered their flags halfway, out of respect. The Father of American revolution was buried in a plain wooden box, just as he had asked.

Glossary

Bill of Rights   document that promises certain rights to people who live in the United States

colony   group of people who move to another land but are still ruled by the same country they moved from. People who live in a colony are called *colonists*.

Continental Congress   group of men that spoke and acted for the colonies that became the United States. It was formed to deal with complaints about Great Britain.

Declaration of Independence   document that said the United States was an independent nation, not under the control or rule of another person or government

Hebrew   language of the Jewish people

Latin   language spoken by the Romans

patriot   person who has great loyalty to his or her country

politics   art or science of government

protest   standing, walking, or making noise in a public place to show disagreement with something

regiment   group of soldiers that is part of a large army

representative   person who is chosen to act or speak for a group of people

Revolutionary War   war from 1775 to 1783 in which North American colonies won their independence from Great Britain

sue   to take someone to court

tavern   place where people could go to eat, drink, and talk

tax   money people must pay to the government

More Books to Read

Heinrichs, Ann. *Samuel Adams*. Chanhassen, Minn.: Child's World, 2004.

Kallen, Stuart A. *Samuel Adams*. Minneapolis, Minn.: ABDO, 2001.

An older reader can help you read these books:

Davis, Kate. *Samuel Adams*. San Diego: Blackbirch, 2002.

Fradin, Dennis. *Samuel Adams*. New York: Clarion Books, 1998.

Place to Visit

Freedom Trail
Boston National Historical Park Visitors' Center
15 State Street
Boston, MA 02109
Visitor Information: (617) 242-5642

Index